C.S. LEWIS

University Press
Copyright © 2019
All Rights Reserved
Cover Image:
Clive Staples Lewis, 1948

Table of Contents

Introduction
Chapter 1: A Book-Filled Childhood
Chapter 2: School and Atheism
Chapter 3: Ireland to England
Chapter 4: World War I and A Promise To Paddy
Chapter 5: Life with Jane
Chapter 6: Turning Towards Theism
Chapter 7: Embracing Christianity
Chapter 8: Academia and Honors
Chapter 9: World War II
Chapter 10: Friends and Societies
Chapter 11: A Marriage of Convenience?
Chapter 12: Master Storyteller
Chapter 13: Nonfiction Writings
Chapter 14: Christian Apologist
Chapter 15: Fame and Charity
Chapter 16: Illness, Death, and Legacy
Conclusion

Introduction

C.S. Lewis is one of the most beloved authors of modern times. People who know little about the man beyond his most famous writings - especially young people – often imagine Lewis as an attractive and charismatic person. Once they see his photo, they are usually disappointed, because he was an ordinary-looking man. Even at the time in his life when he was most famous, he went around in wrinkled slacks, tattered jackets, and worn-out shoes. He was overweight, balding, and not particularly good-looking.

What Lewis's dull outward appearance failed to reveal was his intelligent mind and his vivid imagination. Best known today for his masterpiece *The Chronicles of Narnia*, Lewis was a prolific author as well as a speaker and, eventually, an evangelistic one.

Lewis left Christianity in his youth and turned to atheism, only to make the spiritual journey back through theism to Christianity in his later years.

Along the way, he became perhaps the most well-known Christian apologist of all time.

In fact, most critics, including friends and fellow academicians, saw *The Chronicles of Narnia* as a Christian allegory. Lewis adamantly opposed this view. Others saw his fervent Christian lifestyle as outdated or unbecoming an academic. He could not have cared less, and kept the faith for reasons of the heart and the mind together.

Both a military man and a philanthropist, what Lewis seemed to want most in life was to serve humankind. When he was offered one of the highest awards, he turned it down. Moreover, when he finally became prosperous, he gave his money away. Here was a man who lived his principles joyfully.

Although Lewis never lived a life of luxury, he mingled with literary greats. He met Yeats and shared a long-standing friendship with J.R.R. Tolkien. He rose to the top of his profession without accepting either the fortune or all the honors life presented to him.

Chapter 1

A Book-Filled Childhood

On November 29, 1898, Clive Staples Lewis began a lifetime journey that would take him from an ordinary child to a scholar, an evangelist, and a master storyteller. He was born on that November day in Belfast, Ireland, to Albert James Lewis, a solicitor, and Florence Augusta Lewis, the daughter of an Anglican priest. Albert and Flora had one other child, an older brother to Clive, named Warren Hamilton Lewis. Warren and Clive would be close throughout their lives.

When Clive was very young, he had a dog named Jacksie. Unfortunately, Jacksie was run over by a car when Clive was just four years old. Clive proclaimed that from then on, his own name would be Jacksie, and he refused to answer unless his parents called him that. Eventually, the name was shortened to Jack. It was a name that stuck with him for the rest of his life, at least among those who knew him well.

The Lewis home was filled to brimming with books. There were books stacked double-high in bookshelves, books on tables, books in every nook and cranny of the house. Jack's parents never limited what books he could read. They were all fair game to him, and he read voraciously.

Jack especially liked books with animals that spoke and acted like humans. He was fascinated with the Beatrix Potter stories. At a very early age, he began writing and illustrating his own animal stories. He and Warren also created an imaginary world where animals ruled. They developed a long and complex history for this world, which they called Boxen.

In 1905, Warren was sent off to boarding school. That same year, the family moved to the outskirts of Belfast. Jack spent more and more time reading and less time with other people. Three years later, his mother died from cancer. Jack was ten years old when he lost her. He was grief-stricken and retreated farther into the world of books, still favoring anthropomorphic animal stories, along with a new interest in knights.

Jack's father never recovered from the loss of his wife, who had died on his birthday on August 23, 1908. What was left of the Lewis family was now cold and sad. Jack began to believe that the God of the Bible was nothing more than a vague notion. Paradoxically, he was also intensely angry at God for taking his mother.

As a young boy, Jack got his education from a series of private tutors. Soon after his mother's death, his father sent him to Wynyard School in Watford, Hertfordshire, where he joined Warren, who had been there for three years.

Wynyard closed shortly after Jack arrived because there were not enough students to support the school. Jack had given the name "Oldie" to the headmaster, whose actual name was Robert Capron. Throughout his life, Jack would rename almost everyone that meant anything to him at all. Capron was sent to a psychiatric hospital shortly after the school closed.

Nevertheless, Jack had had his introduction to the educational system. Despite the short stay at Wynyard, Jack had found his niche. He would be a scholar. In this pursuit, his journey was just beginning.

Chapter 2

School and Atheism

C.S. Lewis was well on his way to an atheistic view of life when he changed schools and went to Campbell College. His days at that school were numbered, as he had to leave due to respiratory problems. In Malvern, an established health resort, he started going to Cherbourg House, a preparatory school he called "Chartres."

It was at Chartres that his thinking began to follow his feelings of being angry at God and move on to thoughts that there was no God. He found all religions ill-founded and considered Christianity to be one of the worst religions of all. Instead of reading the Bible, he now immersed himself in tales of the occult and mythology. His favorite myths were from ancient Scandinavia.

During his teenage years, Jack became even more convinced of the wisdom of atheism. He delved into Norse mythology, finding it awoke a sense of wonder and joy within him. He came to revere nature but found this new interest wholly compatible with his atheistic views.

Fellow students remarked on his brilliant style of atheism, saying he was entertaining when laying out his arguments. However, Jack's inner life was darker and more troubled than any of them imagined. He refused to believe in things he could not see and found only meaninglessness in the things he could see and touch. To Jack, the world was a sad and bitter place.

Feeling dissatisfied with the school, he transferred to Malvern College and then left school altogether to study privately with William T. Kirkpatrick. Kirkpatrick had been Jack's father's tutor years ago and, in the meantime, had spent some years as headmaster of Lurgan College. Jack, still always renaming the people and places in his life, called Kirkpatrick "The Great Knock." Kirkpatrick had already been successful in preparing Jack's brother Warnie to enter the Royal Military Academy at Sandhurst, and the hope was that he could do the same for Jack.

During this phase of his life, Jack's imagination grew to become wondrous and alive. He imagined scenes of the divine, yet his reason told him that it was all woven into a fabric of lies. He was in anguish, more because of this disharmony than because of his atheistic views alone.

While studying with Kirkpatrick, Jack learned the fine points of debate and developed his intellectual reasoning. When he emerged from his studies with The Old Knock, he was a masterful student and speaker.

Lewis went to University College, Oxford, to take an exam that would win him a scholarship to the prestigious school. He succeeded, and in 1916, he won the scholarship award. He moved happily to Oxford, ready to learn and meet some of the greatest writers and poets of his day. Still, Ireland was his first love. Even in England, he would not abandon his home.

Chapter 3

Ireland to England

When C.S. Lewis first arrived in England, the way he felt could only be described as culture shock. While people outside the United Kingdom may feel that England and Ireland are similar since they are parts of the same country, Jack found that the English behaved and lived much differently than the Irish people he had known.

Jack turned the wrong way when getting off the train and headed into a dismal housing area. He was extremely disappointed with England at that moment and wondered if he had made the right choice. Just then, he turned around and saw the spires of Oxford. With his mood lightened considerably, he made his way to the university.

Once there, Jack made many friends. His dearest friends, though, were fellow Irishmen who were living at Oxford. He often joked with these companions about the English way of doing things. He continually gave the English ironic compliments, indicating that if only Irishmen knew how to do things like the English, the world would be a better place. Then, he would smile with amusement, giving away the joke.

Jack admired poet W.B. Yeats, not only for his talent but also because his works were a part of the Celtic Revival movement that celebrated his own Irish heritage. Jack intended to find a Dublin publisher and add his own works to the movement, but before he got that far, he began to stray from his Celtic roots.

Although Jack lived the better part of the rest of his life at Oxford, he returned to Northern Ireland often. The turmoil he saw in Belfast between the Protestants and Catholics influenced the way he looked at Christianity later on. He wanted all the people of his beloved home city to live peacefully together, and he extended this desire to all the different brands of Christianity.

In 1921, Lewis had the good fortune of meeting Yeats. He was thoroughly impressed with his fellow Irishman. Nevertheless, he found that others at Oxford ignored Yeats. This was something he never understood, neither at the time he met Yeats nor later in life. He wondered if his love of Yeats' work had something to do with the fact that he himself was Irish and could thus relate better to Yeats' poems. In any case, Yeats has been a revered poet throughout the English-speaking world since before his time at Oxford.

Still, Lewis enjoyed his time at Oxford, socializing with like-minded writers and philosophers. But his time there was brief, at least for the time being. He was shipped off to be a World War I soldier for Britain. He would return to Oxford eventually, but, in the meantime, he felt he had a duty to serve.

Chapter 4

World War I and A Promise to Paddy

C.S. Lewis and all the Lewis family assumed that he would spend at least a part of his life in the military. During World War I, Jack got his chance to serve. He may have imagined battles to be noble and glorious, especially after reading the tales of gallantry he had been so fond of as a young boy.

Three years after World War I started, Jack joined the British Army. He trained at Keble College, Oxford, to be an officer. Training near his Oxford pals, he sometimes got chances to sit and talk with them. Still, his training took up most of his time and energy.

At Keble, Jack's roommate was Edward Courtney Francis Moore. Everyone knew Edward as "Paddy." Jack and Paddy developed a close friendship. They even promised each other that if one of them did not return from the war, the other would take care of his family. They were very serious in this intention, a fact which Jack would have a chance to prove later on.

If Lewis imagined battle to be glorious, the reality of war was quite different than he expected. Over and over, he was appalled by the horrors of the war and the damage it did to people, property, and even the earth itself. World War I was a brutal war, and Lewis was not a violent person by nature.

So, perhaps it was a blessing to him that he received a brief respite from the war after being hit by shards from a mortar shell and severely wounded during the Battle of Arras. If a blessing, it was a mixed one. His father never visited him, and he fell into depression. The only friend he could rely on was his old roommate, Paddy. Paddy also introduced Jack to his mother, and he began what would turn out to be a close friendship with the woman. His recuperation period was short, though, and soon he was returned to active duty. He was discharged soon afterward.

In his autobiography, *"Surprised by Joy: The Shape of My Early Life,"* Lewis described the first bullet he heard in the war and said that, at that moment, he knew he was in a war. He finally understood what Homer was writing about in his famous battle scenes.

Yet, Lewis believed then and later that a just war was ultimately good. Years later, when he wrote *The Chronicles of Narnia*, he portrayed a just war with a glorious ending. Despite his horror at the violence of war, he always believed that there were times when it was necessary. He even spoke at a gathering of pacifists at one point to discuss why he rejected pacifism later in life, publishing the speech in 1940 as *"Why I Am Not a Pacifist."*

In addition to Jack's physical injury, the war deepened his commitment to his atheistic views. After all, how could a Supreme Being be so unjust as to create a world where such violence was necessary? Lewis continued to write during the war, penning a set of poems that at once expressed his atheism and revealed his anger towards a God that might have existed. The poems were published in his first book, *Spirits in Bondage: A Cycle of Lyrics*, in 1919.

While World War I was a traumatic period in Jack's life, it was even more devastating when his friend Paddy was killed on the battlefield in 1918. Jack had a promise to keep. He would look after Paddy's mother and her daughter for as long as they needed him. He returned to Oxford to continue his studies, but this time he was not alone. Very soon after he arrived, Paddy's mother Jane joined him.

Chapter 5

Life with Jane

Although C.S. Lewis and Jane Moore lived together for many years, their relationship was a strange one. Jack always introduced Jane as his mother and called her mother in the letters he wrote during that time. Yet, they shared the same house, which was named "The Kilns," and had rooms situated next to each other.

At least two of Lewis's biographers have speculated that Jane and Jack had a long-running affair. One of the two, George Sayer, knew Jack for over 29 years and felt sure that Jack had consummated his relationship with Paddy's mother soon after they moved in together.

When they met, Jane was gorgeous at age 45. Jack was a brash 18-year-old soldier. Rumors began flying at Oxford that the two of them were a couple in every sense of the word. This was an outrage to many who heard the rumors. How could a fine, intellectual, Oxford gentleman be involved with a woman so much older than him, and one that was not in academia?

Jack appeared not to care about the rumors. He continued to praise Jane's kindness and told friends it was she who taught him compassion towards others. If that is so, he learned his lesson very well. For the rest of his life, he always sought to help the less fortunate.

In her later years, Jane began suffering from dementia. Jack took care of her as long as he could. When he could no longer manage her at the Kilns, he arranged for her to go to a nursing home. Then, he visited her there every day until she died in 1951.

Other men might have dismissed a wartime promise to a friend as a product of the moment and not a lifetime commitment. Jack, though, was a supremely honorable man and always tried to fulfill his promises.

Was there something more to their relationship? It seems likely that there was, but without the promise, Jane probably would not have joined him at the Kilns to live the rest of her life with him. Lewis would have taken care of her in any case, because that was his nature. Still, he was a man who felt joy whenever he found someone whom he thought of as good and kind. He welcomed them into his inner circle with pleasure. And, when the person was a woman, he found even greater joy.

Although the probability seems high that their relationship was healthy both physically and emotionally, the exact extent of it will probably never be known to any degree of certainty. However, one thing that can be said about Jane is that she had a strong effect on his religious views. Suddenly, there was more to life than dismal meaninglessness. He had found a companion that lightened his emotional load, opened him to positivity, and possibly helped turn him from his atheism. He did not jump immediately to Christianity. That would come later. First, he delved into theism.

Chapter 6

Turning Towards Theism

Life had been chipping away at Lewis's commitment to atheism for many years. Jack was always a man who explored philosophical subjects and reasoned his way to a definite conclusion. So, when the subject of evolution became a hot topic, as always, he thought about it until he came to a firm belief as to its validity. It was that conclusion that turned him towards theism.

Theism did not immediately transform Lewis into a Christian. He certainly believed there was an intelligent design to the universe, a god that made the earth and heavens, if not in one literal day, perhaps in a metaphorical one.

While he believed wholeheartedly in the truth and value of science, he found it limited. It could only truly verify what was evident to the five senses. He eschewed scientism, which he saw as a cultish following of scientific study without regard to the powers of mind.

As Lewis saw it, the mind had to be more than a product of the brain. If the mind was just an outgrowth of biology, there was no explanation for why there were so many different and complex ideas, regardless of how the thinkers of those thoughts were physically endowed.

While evolutionists supported the idea that the DNA of a single-celled organism was no different in kind than the DNA of a human, Lewis found this explanation led to the belief that life was meaningless. While he had once been on board with that view, he had now learned from life that some joys and pleasures were significant to him. Love, friendship, and learning, to his mind, went far beyond the biological. There was something holy about them for him.

Once this respect for the divine and holy in the world took hold of Lewis, he began to study books from various religions. He still did not believe in the Jesus of Christianity in the way he would later. At this point, he believed that Jesus was a mythical figure, similar to the gods he had been reading about since he was a young boy.

In other words, it was a good story, but not one based on any kind of spiritual reality.

On one occasion, Jack found himself turning from the occult as he witnessed what looked like a demon possession. Jack's roommate Paddy had an uncle who was wounded in World War I. The man, John Askins, had delved heavily into spiritualism and the occult. When Jack saw him writhing on the floor, crying out that he was being tormented by devils, Jack was deeply affected. Jack's reason told him that the cause of the outbreak was physical and psychological, but emotionally, he found it quite distressing.

Jack loved to debate nearly any topic on which he could shine his intellectual light. Theism was no different in that respect. Before, he had complex but logical arguments for atheism. Now, he refuted that belief and developed strong arguments for its inadequacies as a world view.

During his time as a theist, Lewis opened up more to the beauty in life. Where before he had seen beauty in the rugged wilderness, now he saw beauty in the lives of good and noble people he had met. He often spoke to friends about his theistic views, enjoying the debates, and learning from them at the same time. However, theism was just a short stop on Lewis's spiritual journey. A conversation with a friend helped him to turn the next corner into Christianity.

Chapter 7

Embracing Christianity

J.R.R. Tolkien was a good friend to C.S. Lewis. The two had long conversations about the meaning of life as well as other philosophical topics and, of course, literature. Tolkien was a devout Catholic, so naturally, his arguments tended to favor Christianity. Lewis stuck to his theistic views for a long time, but eventually, Tolkien's views made a more considerable impression on him.

Although Lewis built arguments and then presented them confidently, he also listened and learned from others. He often revised his arguments to take in new insights. While others might stagnate in set beliefs, Tolkien's religious views were always evolving. His changes did not come easily. He grappled with new ideas until he knew them inside and out. Only then would he change his views. But, when he changed, it was a complete conversion to the new belief system.

In the same way, he began struggling to understand the true meaning of Christianity.

Jack took a long train ride and, as always, bought himself a book to read on the way. This time, the book was George Macdonald's *Phantastes*. As he read, he felt a sense of divine holiness coming from the pages to spark his imagination with light once again.

Jack's reasoning began to take a turn also. He read G.K. Chesterton's The Everlasting Man and was impressed with its humor. He also began to think that "Christianity was very sensible apart from its Christianity."

His friends may have had the most influence on turning Jack towards Christianity. Hugo Dyson, Neville Coghill, and in particular, J.R.R. Tolkien, were friends who shared Jack's intellectual passions but were also devout Christians.

One night, some of the friends were sitting around discussing deep subjects, as they usually did when they were together relaxing. Tolkien spoke very persuasively about the validity of the Christian faith. The friends decided to take a car ride that night. Tolkien kept arguing his case through the ride and then through the rest of the night. By morning, Lewis was convinced.

But it was more than an intellectual understanding. Jack had been drawn to something for a long time. Not knowing quite what it was, Jack had experienced it as a pulling towards some great joy. When he fell on his knees and admitted that "God is God," the joy finally exploded into his being. He was a converted man and would remain faithful to Christianity, Jesus, and God for the rest of his life.

Still, it took Lewis another two years to abandon theism completely and transform his life into that of a Christian. By the time the two years were over, he was a member of the Church of England. He stopped writing poems and began creating works that reflected his newfound faith. Lewis's view of religion had changed dramatically. His Christian books would sell millions of copies, but his primary focus was always on academia. He was a scholar first, foremost, and forever.

Chapter 8

Academia and Honors

During his time at Oxford, which encompassed his entire adult life, C.S. Lewis was a man who reasoned from cold, dispassionate logic. He won many informal debates with his fellow scholars, a group that included several writers who are still popular today. He wrote fiction, and especially after his conversion to Christianity, he wrote nonfiction works that laid out compelling arguments for Christianity. Many who read his books were converted.

But, Jack's business was academia. The book-writing was a part of being an academician for him, but it was only a part. He started college in 1917 during the summer term. After spending most of 1918 in the Army, he went back to Oxford to continue his studies. He graduated from that University in 1925, winning a "triple first," the highest honors in three areas of study. Then, it was off to Magdalene College to accept a teaching position on fellowship.

Between and after World Wars I and II, Lewis was a confirmed academic. He was known as a kind but intelligent teacher who challenged his students to learn the fine points of literature and produce excellent work. He helped his students develop rhetorical skills and taught them to question what they read during their studies.

In 1951, King George VI named Lewis to become a Member of the Order of the British Empire. This was a prestigious honor, and it was a great honor even to be considered for it. However, Lewis turned down the position. He did not want to be involved in politics, and he felt that being a member of that order would mar his reputation as an independent thinker, speaker, and writer.

Jack also enjoyed studying Medieval and Renaissance literature. In fact, in 1955, he became the chair of a new department for that very branch of knowledge at Magdalene College. Magdalene welcomed him with open arms and gave him the honor and recognition that Oxford never had.

Lewis had started teaching at Magdalene College, Cambridge, in 1954. Although he was well-respected at Cambridge, he still considered Oxford his academic home. Every weekend, he went to Oxford, where he maintained what he thought of as his primary residence.

In the meantime, Lewis had to choose a path to patriotic service during World War II. While his options were more limited than he would have liked, he had an enormous impact on the people of Britain during the war. World War II could have been his last chance to experience war, but instead, he ended up contributing in more intellectual ways.

Chapter 9

World War II

C.S. Lewis was 41 when he again donned a uniform and took up a rifle to defend Britain. This time, he was a member of the Home Guard, a unit mainly composed of World War I veterans who patrolled the perimeters of the cities. Starting in August 1940, Jack walked around the perimeter of Oxford with two other guards to ensure Germany did not attack innocent civilians.

Everyone called the unit "Dad's Army" and made fun of it often. But the reality is that, given the aggression of the German Army against Britain, his position might well have been crucial had Germany fought a ground war against them.

Lewis did not immediately opt for the Home Guard. First, he tried to go back into service in the regular Army. When he was told that he was too old to fight, he offered to train cadets. Again, he was refused. The only option he was given for active duty in the war was to write for the Ministry of Information. However, he rejected that offer, not wanting to be a part of the propaganda machine – not even for Britain. He simply would not write lies. So, the Home Guard it was.

Jack did agree to speak on radio broadcasts to offer encouragement for the British people, especially during the time the air raids were frequently happening. His speeches were aired on religious broadcasts.

The one thing that stood out more than anything else in the speeches was that he offered the people a reason for being courageous. He developed the idea that what they were going through, how they responded to the war, was deeply meaningful for themselves, for their country, and for the world.

Not long after his service in World War I, Lewis had begun publishing both nonfiction and fiction books and become a well-known, if not quite famous author. His first book, called *Dymer*, was a satire published under the pseudonym, Clive Hamilton. He also used that name for his book *Spirits in Bondage*, also written about the same time. For his 1936 book *The Allegory of Love*, he won the Hawthornden Prize.

Two years later, Lewis released the first of his sci-fi trilogy, *Out of the Silent Planet*. These three sci-fi books had an underlying theme of sin and desire, expressing his religious views through fiction. During World War II, his religious and patriotic speeches became the basis for a collection titled *Mere Christianity*.

Throughout Lewis's time in Oxford and Cambridge, and in World Wars I and II, he was a great patriot, writer, and speaker. He was also a friend to many. He enjoyed spending time in deep conversation with intellectually stimulating friends and acquaintances. In fact, his friendships had a significant influence on his life and works.

Chapter 10

Friends and Societies

C.S. Lewis may have looked like an ordinary man, but his literary abilities proved otherwise. He undoubtedly spent many hours writing. Yet, he also enjoyed the friendships that he made a part of his academic life.

Although Lewis was an atheist when he began college, most of his friends were some brand of Christian or other. J.R.R. Tolkien was one of his closest friends. They shared a passion for learning, and both wrote fantasy books. Yet, their friendship went beyond the merely academic. They were great personal friends throughout their adult lives.

Early in his career at Oxford, Jack joined a group formed by J.R.R. Tolkien called "The Coalbiters." The group discussed Icelandic mythology. Later, an undergraduate named Edward Tangye Lean started a group called "The Inklings" around 1931 at University College, Oxford. The group functioned the same way current-day literary critique circles do. The members brought unfinished works to the meetings and read them aloud. When one read, the others commented on the writing, asking questions, pointing out deficiencies, and pointing out passages that worked well.

Lean left the university two years later, and the Inklings disbanded. Two members of the group, Tolkien and Lewis, started a group by the same name at Magdalene College, where Lewis was teaching at that time.

The Inklings still functioned the same way as it had before. They met every Thursday at Lewis's room and sometimes again on Tuesdays at various pubs. Their favorite was officially named the Eagle and Child, but everyone called it the Bird and the Baby. The Inklings, like many intellectual societies of its day, was an all-male group.

Serious literature was being discussed at the meetings, including Tolkien's *"Lord of the Rings"* and Lewis's *"Out of the Silent Planet."* But they also had fun. They had a custom of reading the work of a female writer named Amanda McKittrick Ros, whom they all considered to be a terrible writer. The trick was to read as long as they could without breaking out laughing.

Lewis was also in a more serious discussion group called the Oxford Socratic Club. This club was formed in 1941 and began meeting in 1942 with Lewis as its first president. The goal of the Socratic Club was to put the Socratic Method to work as they discussed religion, particularly Christianity, in terms of its relationship to the intellect. The Socratic club discussed philosophical positions, including the apparent clash between science and religion was one of the hottest topics at the Socratic Club.

Members of the club read papers, and others responded. Members of the club included Iris Murdoch, Dorothy L. Sayers, C.E.M. Joad, I.M. Crombie, Elizabeth Anscombe, and J.L. Austin. Great debates about the papers and related themes often resulted between members of the club.

One of the more famous debates in the Socratic Club was between Lewis and Elizabeth Anscombe. Anscombe was a Catholic philosopher who challenged Lewis's view that arguments for naturalism failed. He first presented this view in his book *"Miracles."* His point was that if nature was created by chance, then it was impossible for the brain to produce anything but chance perceptions and ideas.

Anscombe refuted Lewis's argument, saying that he had confused a non-logical nature of reality with an illogical nature. Lewis was so affected by losing the debate that he went back to *Miracles* and made changes to bolster his argument.

All this social/intellectual contact suited Lewis very well, but he did not confine his relationships to Oxford or Cambridge academics. Late in life, he began a relationship with a woman who came to him with her own intellectual gifts.

Chapter 11

A Marriage of Convenience?

Many people in Oxford thought of Lewis as a man who preferred the company of men. Some even referred to him as a misogynist and said he would go out of his way to avoid being near women. However, the facts of his life are much different. After caring for Paddy's mother, Jane, Lewis had another special relationship with a woman that lasted as long as she lived.

In 1950, C.S. Lewis discovered that he had two enthusiastic young fans. The young boys' mother, Joy Gresham, began writing to Lewis about her sons' love of his *Chronicles of Narnia*. Lewis and Gresham began corresponding with each other and proved to be an intellectual match. Joy sparked his imagination and challenged his mind. At that point, the attraction was not romantic; but still, it was intense.

Joy was contending with William Gresham, her abusive, alcoholic husband, but her interest in

Lewis took her mind off her destructive relationship. In 1952, she flew to Oxford to get a glimpse of Lewis and try to meet him. As the story goes, she went to a men's club in Oxford to find him. Not knowing what he looked like, she called out his name until he went to her to find out who she was.

Two years later, Joy's husband went too far. He wanted Joy to take part in a ménage au trois with his mistress. Disgusted, she divorced him and left him for good. She also had to deal with the fact that she would not be allowed to stay in England any longer as a non-citizen. But, Lewis solved that problem suggesting that if they were married, she would not have to leave.

In 1956, Jack and Joy were married. Joy had a sense of humor that matched Jack's, while they could also connect on intellectual ideas and issues. Finally, there was a woman he could talk to as an equal while thoroughly enjoying her company. They also had come through similar religious journeys, both moving through atheism to Christianity.

Others at Oxford talked disparagingly about the relationship between Jack and Joy. After all, she was part Jewish, an American and a former communist – not the sort of person they thought would be a fitting companion to the beloved Lewis. However, Jack disagreed. He ignored the controversy and focused on his love of this beautiful and intelligent woman.

Joy and Jack lived happily until she began to have extreme pain in her hip. She was diagnosed with bone cancer and nearly died. At that point, Jack and Joy's relationship became closer and more romantic than it had been before. While the first marriage had only been a civil union, they now wanted a religious ceremony. Because Joy was divorced, the Church of England resisted allowing the marriage. However, a friend who was a minister married them at her bedside in 1957.

Miraculously, Joy's cancer went into remission. Jack and Joy greeted the news with pleasure, spending the next three years reveling in each other's company. They lived with Jack's brother Warnie. In 1960, Joy's cancer returned. Jack took her on a tour of Greece, a fact that shows how deeply he loved her, because he hated to travel. She died on July 13, 1960.

When Joy died, Lewis was heartbroken. He wrote a book about the grieving process he went through, including his anger, sadness, and near despair. He published this book, *"A Grief Observed,"* under the pen name N.W. Clerk to avoid revealing his anguish to the general public. This pen name was so effective at hiding the author's true identity that friends suggested that Lewis read the book to help him deal with the loss of his wife. The book was not published under Lewis's name until after his death.

Lewis was distraught for a time, but he was never one to wallow in sadness. He still wrote, participated in The Inklings and the Socratic Club, and maintained close contact with his social circle. He also raised Joy's sons, Douglas and David. Douglas became a Christian, but David took up his mother's early faith and embraced Judaism.

Through relationships and losses, through all the religious wanderings and intellectual interests in his life, Lewis continually produced new writings. His Narnia stories have become children's classics, read and admired by people of all ages. Yet, the *Chronicles of Narnia* were not his only fiction books. He was a prolific writer who tapped into his magnificent imagination to enthrall readers of his time and delight his most faithful readers even until the current time.

Chapter 12

Master Storyteller

C.S. Lewis's childhood stories of the imaginary world of Boxen gave but a glimpse of the master storyteller he would later become. At first, his prose was not well-received, but later stories thrilled his readers then as they do now.

Lewis wrote his first work of fiction on a two-week vacation. The book, *Pilgrim's Regress*, was published in 1933. The story told in this book is based loosely on John Bunyan's *Pilgrim's Progress*. It is an allegory that describes a search for an island of Desire. The protagonist, John the pilgrim, travels a landscape filled with political and philosophical dangers. The book addresses issues of the day, such as the growing movement of fascism. He meets a fellow traveler named Mr. Vertue, and the two navigate their world, still searching for the island.

Pilgrim's Regress was something of a literary disaster. The critics of his day panned it, and he sold very few copies. It was passed from publisher to publisher. Lewis had made obscure references that his readers did not understand, so in the third edition, he wrote a lengthy preface and added chapter headings to help elucidate the meanings.

Lewis might have given up on writing fiction had he not received support and encouragement from an Oxford friend, David Lloyd-Jones. When his friend asked him when he would write fiction again, he said that he would only take on another fiction book when he understood prayer.

Later on, Lewis had several conversations with his good friend J.R.R. Tolkien about the nature of current science fiction. They agreed that the sci-fi stories of the day left out the moral struggles people would face in these futuristic worlds. They decided to write their own sci-fi novels that would fulfill this purpose. Tolkien was to write a book about time travel. He started it never finished.

Lewis, on the other hand, did finish and publish his work on space travel, called the *Space Trilogy* or *Cosmic Trilogy*. The first, *Out of the*

Silent Planet, was published in 1938, the second in 1943, and the third in 1945. The first book is set on Mars, the second on Venus, and the third on Earth.

The hero of the first two books of the Space Trilogy stories is Elwin Ransom, a philologist who, like Lewis, was an expert in medieval literature and had only one living relative. In the first book, Ransom finds out that Earth has been exiled from the rest of the solar system and is now under the influence of an angel named Bent Oyarsa.

The second book reveals humanity just emerging on Venus. The third book, in which Ransom is a less central character, tells the story of a think tank on Earth that is in touch with demonic forces. All three books make use of the Old Solar language, created by Lewis and similar to Tolkien's Elvish languages. The books also use various ancient figures from Tolkien's mythology, as well as ancient Greek and Norse mythologies. After the *Space Trilogy* was completed, Lewis began another manuscript that featured Elwin Ransom. Lewis never finished this book, but it was published in 1977.

The Chronicles of Narnia are, by far, Lewis's most well-known and popular works. Although they are written for children, the complexity of the stories and the vivid depictions of an imaginary world have fascinated adults as well.

The 7-book series includes:
1. The Lion, the Witch, and the Wardrobe, published in 1950.
2. Prince Caspian: The Return to Narnia, published in 1951.
3. The Voyage of the Dawn Treader, published in 1952.
4. The Silver Chair, published in 1953.
5. The Horse and His Boy, published in 1954.
6. The Magician's Nephew, published in 1955.
7. The Last Battle, published in 1956.

The only character to appear in all seven books is Aslan, the Great Lion. Lewis has described Aslan as his answer to what Jesus would have been like if he had been set in this imaginary world. He refutes the idea that the Chronicles of Narnia are allegorical, saying that they are stories about a possible alternative reality that would happen under the circumstances described in the book. The books feature mythological themes from a variety of sources, as well as references to occultism and paganism. Yet, the Christian themes are predominant in the *Chronicles*.

Critics of the *Chronicles* have suggested that the stories are gender-biased and racist. It is clear the women have different roles than men in the stories and that fictional people similar to Muslims are not treated fairly. Whether Lewis was aware of the significance of these choices is unclear but is in keeping with the cultural norms of his day. Still, with a man as moral and gifted in storytelling as Lewis, one might expect more.

The Chronicles of Narnia have been among the bestselling books of modern times. They have sold more than 100 million copies in 41 languages, and they have become a cultural phenomenon that continues to have an impact today.

Other books include The Great Divorce, a story about inhabitants of Hell who take a bus ride to Heaven, where they can choose to stay but decide they do not like it there. The Screwtape Letters has also been a well-known Lewis novel. It is a series of fictional letters from a demon to his nephew. His final book was Till We Have Faces, which tells the story of Psyche and Cupid in Christian terms.

Despite all these tributes to Lewis's imagination, many of his books were nonfiction works. Lewis was fond of developing and presenting arguments, both in face-to-face debates and in literary form. His nonfiction books gave him an excellent opportunity to do just that.

Chapter 13

Nonfiction Writings

C.S. Lewis is best known for his fiction and the *Chronicles of Narnia* in particular. But the truth is that Lewis penned far more nonfiction than fiction. The main topics of his nonfiction relate either to his religious journey or to his studies and teachings as a scholar and professor.

His first nonfiction book on a scholarly subject was *The Allegory of Love: A Study in Medieval Tradition*, which was published in 1936. In 1948, Lewis wrote on Charles Williams' poetry in a work called *Arthurian Torso*. He contributed an entry on Edmund Spenser to *Major British Writers, Vol. I* in 1954. His 1964 volume called *The Discarded Image: An Introduction to Medieval and Renaissance Literature*, was his last published academic book. He wrote much about language itself, including *Studies in Words*, 1960. He also wrote prefaces for several literary works during his time as a professor.

Lewis spoke and wrote extensively on his Christian views. His collection of radio speeches called *Mere Christianity*, published in 1952, was a compilation of three earlier collections titled *Broadcast Talks*, *Christian Behaviour*, and *Beyond Personality*. His book Miracles, published in 1947, was an argument that miracles can and do happen in the world. This is the book that he revised in 1960 after debating about its subject with G.E.M. Anscombe during a Socratic Club meeting.

Other Christianity-focused books include *The Problem of Pain*, in which Lewis argues that pain and hell are not good enough reasons to reject the notion of God, *The Case for Christianity*, and *Reflections on the Psalms*. His *Letters to Malcolm: Chiefly on Prayer* was published in 1964.

In 1958, C.S. Lewis spoke in radio broadcasts about love from both Christian and philosophical viewpoints. American listeners complained that the talks were too explicit and included too much open discussion of sexual matters. However, these talks were compiled in a book called *The Four Loves*, published in 1960. He defines his four versions of love as Storge, an empathy bond, Philia, a friend bond, Eros, an erotic bond, and Agape, God's love.

In two of his most passionate nonfiction writings, Lewis tells his own story. His *Surprised by Joy: The Shape of My Early Life*, Lewis tells the story of his boyhood longing for joy and his rediscovery of the Christian faith after years as an atheist. *A Grief Observed* was a compelling description of the grieving process based on his own personal loss when his wife Joy died.

All of these writings contributed to Lewis's fame in academic circles and even in the general public. The Christian writing, in particular, was a part of his commitment to Christian apologetics, a field in which he became known as a primary contributor.

Chapter 14

Christian Apologist

C.S. Lewis was a leading Christian apologist of his day. Even now, many people know little about Christian apologetics except for Lewis's name. His goal was to present logical arguments for Christianity that any reasonable person could understand and accept.

Since the early years of the Christian movement, apologists from the Apostle Paul to Thomas Aquinas to C.S. Lewis have defended the religion. Christian apologists traditionally base their arguments on historical and scientific evidence as well as philosophical ideas. Modern apologists like Lewis have also referred to many different academic disciplines to prove their points.

Lewis's *Mere Christianity* became a classic in Christian apologetics nearly as soon as the radio broadcasts from which it was taken were aired. While early apologetics sought to integrate

Christian values into the Roman culture and ideology, Lewis aimed to reach skeptics who did not want to believe in Christianity without first examining its premises. Lewis was especially interested in appealing to academics who had rejected Christianity as an illogical choice.

In his early college days, before he returned to Christianity, Lewis read extensively from the works of G.K. Chesterton, who wrote about 80 books in his lifetime. Chesterton fascinated Lewis because of his unique combination of intelligence, wit, and Christian ideals. The Chesterton work that influenced Lewis the most was *The Everlasting Man*, which Lewis later said had "baptized his imagination." Reading from the books of this famous Christian apologist became a significant turning point in Lewis's religious experience.

Later, Lewis himself argued the logic and rationality of believing in the Christian faith. His famous trilemma was an argument that stated that Jesus had to be divine if he was not deluded or evil. For this reason, according to the trilemma, Jesus could not be considered just a wise teacher, but must have in some way been God.

Surprisingly, many theologians and biblical scholars reject Lewis's trilemma. They reason that Jesus, in fact, never claimed to be God. He merely pointed the way to the divine kingdom of God. Some may feel that Jesus had a special relationship with the God of Israel, but most stop short of agreeing with Lewis's position that Jesus was and is divine.

Lewis, though, wanted to prove his own belief that Jesus proclaimed His divinity by the claims He made even though He may never have said outright that He was God. Jesus claimed to have the authority to forgive sins, something that Lewis assumed only God could do. Jesus also claimed He had always existed, which, if true, would make him immortal, like God is. He also claimed that He would come back to judge the world when time came to an end.

While Lewis did not invent the trilemma argument, he argued it more forcefully, and to a larger crowd, than early evangelists had. Of course, Lewis's trilemma drew criticism from those who were not Christians, but it was also not accepted by all religious people. Some said that Jesus' words could have been twisted by his followers, who wrote down the accounts of his life. In that case, he might not have made any claims to divinity, but it might all have been legend rather than fact.

A part of Lewis's Christian apologetics was based on his understanding of universal morality, which has also been referred to before and after his time as Natural Law. Natural or Universal Law is simply the right and wrong that all people recognize and try to encourage in their peers. Lewis argues that all people are well aware of this universal morality and choose whether or not to abide by it.

Most importantly, Lewis argues that for there to be such a law, recognized by everyone naturally, there must be a great intelligence behind the law. He saw this as the only clear and logical explanation for human behavior – whether in keeping with the law or going against it.

Lewis distinguished common morality from herd instinct and explained in *Mere Christianity* that Natural Law was quite different from social convention. He stated that, even though different people abided by different moral codes, the fact that there are some moral ideas that are deemed better in one society than in another agrees with the argument that there is some Real Morality that each is trying to aspire to.

In any case, Lewis made a name for himself as one of the most talked-about Christian apologists of his time. When his book Miracles was published in 1947, TIME devoted a cover story to Lewis. The accompanying article expressed amazement that a noted scholar such as C.S. Lewis would be audacious enough to go against academia in that way. His works continue to influence Christian apologists today.

Chapter 15

Fame and Charity

C.S. Lewis's rise to fame was not meteoric but gradual and steady. As Lewis spoke about his theological perspectives on the radio and preached sermons in various churches, his popularity grew. His readership also grew from the few people who read and enjoyed his first works to the millions who loved his later works of fiction. Among academics, his nonfiction works became famous for their intellectual treatment of issues that had been handled in primarily emotional ways in the past. Soon, he was a famous figure in English literature.

Jack's income also increased dramatically over those years. Yet, his lifestyle barely changed at all in terms of wealth and luxury. Instead of buying expensive things or going on world tour vacations, he never increased his standard of living. Instead, he wore old clothing and spent little on recreation.

So, where did all the money go? Most of Lewis's money went to the people who needed it. He established a charity with his royalties very early on in his career. He also gave financial support to many needy families. He gave money to orphans and poor seminary students to help them achieve their educational goals. He donated to a large number of charities and helped support church ministries.

Lewis discussed his views on charity in his book *Mere Christianity*. To Lewis, charity was an expression of God's love. It meant loving people in the sense of caring deeply about what happened to them and not in loving them with affection. However, during his life, he nurtured his affections for others, understanding that this would make being charitable to them much easier. Jack could not pinpoint a certain amount of money that he should give to the poor. So, he chose to err on the side of abundance and give more than he could really spare.

Committed to charitable giving, Jack also made many humorous comments about people who chose not to give. For instance, some would say that giving money to a poor drunk was useless because he would only use it to buy liquor.

Lewis's response was, "But if I kept it, I should probably have drunk it."

Lewis's feelings about giving to charity were at once passionate and personal. He rejected the idea that philanthropy should happen at a cold, impersonal distance. Jack reveled in giving to others and seeing that they did well afterward.

He expressed his Christian charity at home as well, as he cared for the people in his life during difficult times. Jane, Joy, and Joy's children all at one time or another relied on him for emotional, financial, and spiritual support. And Jack, being Jack, was happy to supply that support as long and as well as he possibly could.

Chapter 16

Illness, Death, and Legacy

Jack began having kidney problems in June 1961. At that time, doctors discovered that inflammation in his kidneys had caused blood poisoning in his system. Lewis was to teach at Cambridge in the fall, but instead, he had to sit out the semester to recover from his kidney troubles.

In 1962, Jack's condition improved until April, when he was well enough to go back to teaching. By 1963, Lewis appeared as healthy as ever. However, on July 15th of that year, he became so ill he had to be hospitalized. The day after he was admitted to the hospital, he had a heart attack and went into a coma.

Everyone expected that the end was near, but he surprised them all by waking up the next afternoon. He was released from the hospital and returned to his home at the Kilns. He was not well enough to go back to work, though, and he remained at the Kilns. When it became evident that he was not going to recover soon enough to teach at Cambridge the following semester, Jack resigned his professorship in August.

Lewis was diagnosed with end-stage renal disease. By mid-November, he was very ill. On November 22, 1963, he collapsed at his home and died a few minutes later. He was buried at Holy Trinity Church, Headington, Oxford. Ten years later, In 1973, his brother Warnie was buried beside him.

The media virtually ignored Lewis's death. Any other day, he might have been celebrated with widespread media reports and announcements of his funeral. The media attention did not go to Lewis, however. There was a far more shocking news story making the rounds of world newspapers, radio, and television. Lewis had died less than an hour before American President John F. Kennedy was assassinated.

Lewis's books have influenced some of the greatest Christian minds in modern times, as well as great writers from all religions. Several biographies and biographical movies and plays have been produced since his death. Many of his unpublished and unfinished manuscripts were released after he died, thanks to his literary executor Walter Hooper and others.

C.S. Lewis Societies, based on the ideals and methodology of the Inklings, exist around the world. His character Digory from *The Magician's Nephew*, was immortalized in bronze; the statue stands in the Hollywood Arches of Lewis's native Belfast.

On November 22, 2013, the world finally gave Lewis the honors he richly deserved. It was the 50th anniversary of his death, and Lewis was being honored as the newest member of Poets' Corner, Westminster Abbey. During a formal ceremony, a floor stone was placed in Poets' Corner. The inscription on the stone read, "I believe in Christianity as I believe that the Sun has risen, not because I see it, but because, by it, I see everything else."

Conclusion

C.S. Lewis is one of the most beloved children's authors of modern times, writing the Chronicles of Narnia that has long been a children's classic. While he might have looked plain and ordinary to people who saw him but did not know him, he proved himself to be an intellectually gifted thinker and writer during his lifetime.

Lewis's spiritual journey began when he was just a young child going to church with his family. When he turned to atheism, it was at least partly due to the emotional trauma of losing his mother. Yet, he felt he had sound reasons for not believing in God. Later in life, when he returned to Christianity, it was his logic that overrode his earlier arguments rejecting the Christian religion.

In this and throughout his life, Lewis searched for the joy of discovery and insight. A gifted intellectual, Lewis used his imagination together with his rationality to explore scholarly subjects from literature to science. Long before his life was over, Lewis had formed a unique world view that he expressed through both his fiction and nonfiction works.

C.S. Lewis's portrayal of Aslan in the Chronicles of Narnia is a treasured rendition of the Christian concept. At the same time, it has been made and remade into movies and other media as a series of adventure-fantasy stories that have sparked the imaginations of countless children and adults from all walks of life and around the world.

Lewis himself had at least one great love and one great friend. His wife, Joy, brought him laughter, companionship, and romantic love. His friendship with J.R.R. Tolkien helped shape his mind and allowed him to occupy his time with personal warmth and understanding.

Jack Lewis was a man of outstanding personal qualities. Lewis showed his compassion, a gift he says he learned from Paddy's mother Jane, through his generous donations to help the less fortunate. He revealed his reliability as he continued to visit Jane long after she could even recognize him. His genuine concern for all of humanity comes across in his books, his letters, and in the transcripts of his speeches. That is the inspiring legacy of C.S. Lewis.

Made in the USA
Monee, IL
14 November 2020